I CAN'T TALK ABOUT THE TREES
WITHOUT THE BLOOD

PITT POETRY SERIES

ED OCHESTER, EDITOR

I CAN'T TALK ABOUT THE TREES WITHOUT THE BLOOD

TIANA CLARK

UNIVERSITY OF PITTSBURGH PRESS

Published by the University of Pittsburgh Press, Pittsburgh, Pa., 15260

Copyright © 2018, Tiana Clark

All rights reserved

Manufactured in the United States of America

Printed on acid-free paper

10 9 8 7 6 5 4 3

ISBN 13: 978-0-8229-6558-9

Cover art: Terrance Hayes, *I Think Imma' Nina Simone*

Cover design: Alex Wolfe

For Ryan, I see you first and only and always.

Even the trees must perform sorrow.

        Roger Reeves

CONTENTS

II. ABOUT THE TREES

III. WITHOUT THE BLOOD

EPILOGUE

Nashville

is hot chicken on sopping white bread with green pickle
chips—sour to balance prismatic, flame-colored spice
for white people. Or, rather, white people now curate hot
chicken for $16 and two farm-to-table sides, or maybe

they've hungered fried heat and grease from black food
and milk—but didn't want to drive to Jefferson Street or
don't know about the history of Jefferson Street or Hell's
Half Acre, north of downtown. Where freed slaves lived

on the fringe of Union camps, built their own new country.
Where its golden age brought the Silver Streak, a ballroom
bringing Basie, Ellington, and Fitzgerald. First-run movies
at the Ritz and no one had to climb to the balcony. 1968,

they built the interstate. I-40 bisected the black community
like a tourniquet of concrete. There were no highway exits.
120 businesses closed. Ambulance siren driving over
the house that called 911, diminishing howl in the distance,

black bodies going straight to the morgue. At the downtown
library, a continuous loop flashes SNCC videos with black
and white kids training for spit and circular cigarette burns
as the video toggles from coaching to counters covered

in pillars of salt and pie and soda—magma of the movement.
On I-65, there is a two-tone Confederate statue I flick off
daily on my morning commute. Walking down Second Avenue,
past neon Honky Tonks playing bro-country and Cash

and herds of squealing pink bachelorette parties—someone
yelled *Nigger-lover* at my husband. Again. Walking down
Second Avenue, I thought I heard someone yelling at the back
of my husband. I turned around to find the voice and saw

myself as someone who didn't give a damn. Again. I turned
around to find that it was I who lived inside the lovely word
made flesh by white mouths masticating mashed sweet potatoes
from my mother's mother's mother—Freelove was her name,

a slave from Warrior, North Carolina, with twelve children
with names like Pansy, Viola, Oscar, Stella, and Toy—
my grandmother. There is always a word I'm chasing inside
and outside of my body, a word inside another word, scanning

the *OED* for soot-covered roots: 1577, 1584, 1608 . . . Tracing my
finger along the boomerang shape of the Niger River for my blood.
1856, 1866, 1889 . . . *Who said it?* A hyphen—crackles and bites,
burns the body to a spray of white wisps, like when the hot comb,

with its metal teeth, cut close to petroleum jelly edging the scalp—
sizzling. Southern Babel, smoking the hive of epithets hung fat
above bustling crowds like black-and-white lynching photographs,
mute faces, red finger pointing up at my dead, some smiling,

some with hats and ties—all business, as one needlelike lady
is looking at the camera, as if looking through the camera, at me,
in the way I am looking at my lover now—halcyon and constant.
Once my mother-in-law said: *Watch your back,* and I knew exactly

what she meant. Again. I turned around to find I am the breath
of Apollo panting at the back of Daphne's wild hair, chasing words
like arrows inside the knotted meat between my shoulder blades—
four violent syllables stabbing my skin, enamored with pain.

I am kissing all the trees—searching the mob, mumbling to myself:
Who said it?
Who said it?
Who said it?

I. I CAN'T TALK

. . . inside our lives, where we are all caught hanging,
the rope inside us, the tree inside us, its roots our limbs,
a throat sliced through and when we open our mouth
to speak, blossoms, o blossoms, no place coming out . . .

Claudia Rankine

Cross/Bite

I was born into this world sideways.
Doctor said,
surgery, to break my face
set it right again
as if breaking were simple.
Wet places my lips have been:
all the boys I've kissed—
so many caves I've licked
saliva & sweat
holy water on my tongue.
I grind my teeth at night
wake to white sand in my mouth:
nocturnal silt, gritty loam.
My jaws pop when I talk
but if I had the surgery, went cosmetic?
Oh, the typewriter in my bones—
yes, I would miss that click/clack the most.

Cottonmouth

The man's mouth unhinged.

He said *I broke my jaw*
and it open likes this now.

       I heard the wet click
of little bones unfastening.

~

I woke up before anyone else
and walked outside barefoot

to the chilled porch still slick
with a thin layer of morning dew.

There was a little coral snake
asleep, coiled by a rocking chair.

I wasn't afraid this time.

~

We were told the snake
was the most beautiful thing

God created until the snake
wanted to be God or like a god

or godlike. I'm not sure now.

~

It happened again—the same dream.

~

I have seen three women give birth
and with each contraction
the mighty hips break and stretch,
the leathery mouth of a snake.

I watched as they writhed
inside the all-consuming pain, pure as God,
fists clenched, wailing something
not quite human, but animal enough.

~

Once, she dreamt she swallowed
a snake till she *became* the snake—
looping, legless reptile, thick
and aching. She woke up paralyzed
until she shouted *Jesus.* Her arms
grasping the invisible beast, blacking
the dark.

~

The guy with the broken mouth
baptized me once inside a Pentecostal

church. He said I had to be fully
immersed for it to count for heaven,

                              you know.

He said Jesus's name only—
No trinity, just Jesus.

Then he touched me under the water.
Plucked and dripping, I came

to the surface, and I shouted and they shouted.
Everyone's mouths open in praise.

~

The snake hisses like a married man.
He measured and whispered slow

       You better. Get out. Of my car.

In a way that meant *devour*:
to swallow *me* whole—

crystalline sweat stippled across his forehead,
his eyes, feral and glinting like two tiger eye
gemstones. The street glazed with vulgar light.
I felt so vulnerable when the tiny metals
unlatched

from my seatbelt
                 breaking jangled air
                                 with delicious clatter.

I was a *good girl* that night, he later said.

~

Lateral undulation:

We swam in the river until we saw a snake muscling
the skin of the water with mini ripples—making waves, then circles.

~

. . . they shall lick the dust like a serpent,
like the crawling things of the earth . . .

The broken jaw: Eight centimeters now :: *Push! Push!*

~

All I remember about my grandmother
is her pouf of white hair dolloped in her coffin,
a cloudy cotton boll.

I snatch the silver snakes
out of my black wool hair, a juicy Medusa.
Still, I can't wait to be like her—all fog and forgetting.

Am I being eaten, or eating? Who can say, really?

~
So the dream goes something like this:

> a snake slithered   between my legs,
> poured out my   mouth—one long continuous
> loop—glossy   glittering scales—voluminous
> muscle—   elongated might—becoming
> ouroboros   —my body a circle
> becoming   samsara—entering
> and exiting   the holy, holy *O*
> at the center   of my deepening
>   meat.

~
To creep, to crawl. I crawl. My mother licks
the floor with her feet.

I bite John Berryman's tail
and Henry runs out of his mouth.

I crawl inside John Berryman's mouth
and manumit Henry. Now Henry is free.

Henry, you don't have to talk *like that* anymore.

~

What if he wanted to leave
his wife and find another keeled
and granular body? His belly travels
like a snake. She believes her father
is also snake.

~

I have so many dark scars and purpled bruises
on my legs.

I have my mother's knees, crunchy and difficult.
Everything hurts when I'm about to go to sleep.

The snake is ready for me, *shhhhh.*

~

Every time she passes this one motel she shivers
at the things she did with her body to the man

with the mouth of a snake—all his holy,
masculine fire
consuming her—whole, she was taken.

After.

He prayed for forgiveness.   Not from her.
But from God. To make him able and clean again.

She is always in that room

                              on the bed, naked
                              like prey.

~

I've got two fangs   in my mouth   that could pierce you.
My cross-bite never   ground down my teeth.

I used to bite   myself in my sleep, but never drew blood.
I gave birth   to myself—and held myself   there. There.

Bear Witness

after Carrie Mae Weems's Roaming *series*

Before I knew
how to fill my onyx body
with slick measures,

dip every curve
in my skin with dark sway,
I needed a picture.

Before me stood
a long black dress I called *Woman*—
you stand opaque

with your back to me,
a statue of witness,
the door of Yes—

I can Return
to the monument
of your silhouette

to find my longest muscle.
We both stare down
the ocean to stillness.

O, Carrie—
what are you trying
to tell me here?

I've been standing by water
my whole damn life
trying to get saved.

Soil Horizon

. . . the ghost of history lies down beside me,
rolls over, pins me beneath a heavy arm.

∾ Natasha Trethewey

My husband's mother wanted to take the family portrait
at Carnton Plantation. I was the only person she called to ask

if it was okay. She said *We could redeem the land with our picture—*
my brown skin acrostic to the row of their white. She said *Can't we*

just let the past be the past? I was silent, my cell phone glowing
warm against my cheek. I was driving, red light—then go. She said

It's practically in my backyard and that her boys played on buckled
fields of green graves growing up—*There are so many fun places to shoot!*

Oh and that big magnolia is in bloom—fragrant milky petals and waxy
greens by the red brick house, and the large front porch with rocking chairs

tipping back and forth above the purpled stains of Confederate blood. I
said it was fine as long as we weren't by the slave cabins, and she laughed

and I laughed, which is to say I wasn't joking at all. She kept saying:
redeem, as if to say, we'll make it acceptable: restore and atone, buy it

back, pay it off, *we'll redeem it*, she said again. Her voice swelling,
like she was singing, and as if we really could. . . .

How do we stand on the dead and smile? I carry so many black souls
in my skin, sometimes I swear it vibrates, like a tuning fork when struck.

~

A staff officer wrote, "the wounded, in hundreds, were brought to [the house]
during the battle, and all the night after. And when the noble old house could
hold no more, the yard was appropriated until the wounded and dead filled that. . . ."

~

The plantation was named after cairns, prophetic stones marking a mass
grave still speaking. How the body leaves its mark on wood—plum dark

and greasy from the shot stippled and amputated. My tongue was cut off
when she asked me again *Are you sure it's okay?* I was waiting at the red

light, my cell phone burned from the hot battery in my hand. Even the dark
layers of dirt must testify—how the Battle of Franklin turned the farmstead

to a field hospital, thousands of casualties during the war for states' rights
the brochure said, and now it's sold out for summer weddings with mint

juleps in sweating silver cups, cannon bursts from weekend reenactments,
and photo shoots for graduation, pregnant couples, and my new family.

~

It's raining. The photographer is snapping and directing us toward the daffodils,
the shutter opening and closing like a tiny guillotine—clicking.

I'm staring at the black eye, clutching my smile. Light drizzle turning my pressed
hair slowly back to curls, the water percolating—weathering its way down

to the bright green topsoil, fertile with the past: organic and holy, wet as Dixie
myth—mixing with iron, clay, aluminum, and revision—romancing the dirt

and undead, churning the silt in the subsoil, steeping farther down—deep, deep
into the dark pocket of earth, to the parent material, layers of large unbroken rocks,

down to the antebellum base, the bedrock of Southern amnesia. *Can't we just let
the past be the past?* she said. Her voice swelling, like she was singing,

                                                    and as if we really could.

~

In the portrait, my husband is holding my hand—his hand that dug for bullets as a boy.

Conversation with Phillis Wheatley #1

Don't you hate your name?

~

I was named like all things are named:
after the things that carry them. Blacked
out belly of my slave ship, the pitching

womb of the ocean slapped against splint-
ered and swollen wood. My only mother
was born-again darkness slatted with sun

and moonlight. There is no mercy before
this one. How do you cry for a continent
that you cannot smell? I had no ears or nose

before the stench of damp and sour bodies
chained with moaning, calling out in different
tongues to different gods—all midnight babel.

Small and unchained, I slipped through feverish
thighs like a small, soft egg floating inside
the scorching center of this moving hyphen—

African-American: dash exposing the break.

Conversation with Phillis Wheatley #2

Tell me about your baptism she asked.

~

I rose out of the water, a caught fish—slippery,
gaping for breath, brand new with righteousness.

I walked down to the frothing whirlpool,
Pastor Lonnie—a white man in a white robe,

extended his hands and helped me down the steps.
The congregation watched as I answered his questions:

Yes. Yes. Yes. Jacuzzi-warm water gurgled and spun
as his white robe spread around my little circumference,

holy creamer. He put his hand on my nose, pinched
my breath. I did not close my eyes as he buried me

under the water—under the water I heard muffled
shouting, under the water I saw Pastor Lonnie's face

ripple in thirds. He tipped my body back, lifted me up
and out of the wet coffin to the deafening resound

of clapping and yelling from the church. My hair back
to curls, my face like the face of my birth when I was cut

from my mother—terrified, ready to scream.

Conversation with Phillis Wheatley #7

Have you ever been for sale? she asked. *Yes* I said
at the country club for the Eve of Janus Debutante Ball.

~

We were good at hiding our zip code and teeth.
They wanted all white, floor length,

and preferably designer. My mother's best friend
bought the dress on sale from a department store.

It was the kind of dress that looked expensive,
but wasn't—shiny and pure and no one would know.

My mother promised to pay her back at the end
of the month. Same for the dinner—$100 a plate

for some charity. My boyfriend's mother was on
the board of the ball and got me in. They wanted

the name of my father and only his name, kept asking
and prying, reaching inside my little life to lift any lineage

to properly present my fresh body to high society.
They wanted: *Mr. and Mrs. Whiter White III presents . . .*

I gave them the only name I had—my mother's:
Verna Marguerite Knight.

I walked on stage, clean and dreamy as a cloud,
a young girl in transition and paused as the master

of ceremonies stumbled over my data: Black girl.
Um, no father. *Pause.* Mother's full name. *Um,* Senior

in High School (*COUGH*). College plans, etc. . . .
The hot spotlight on my galactic silhouette shot

through me as my blackness blurred over white faces
in the crowd, except for my mother and her best friend

and the servers with thick, lily-white gloves. I walked
down the runway, the auction block. Past the portrait

of Robert E. Lee into the blinding snow-bright circle
of center stage. Half my face split by light, one half caught

in the beam, the other lost inside my shadow smacked
against the wall, looking back on Belle Meade Plantation

at the kitchen's dirty dishes stacked like cairns for my kin,
looking forward into a rich blizzard—a wealthy haze

of glittering tables, clinking china, a flurry of whispers.
Old Money looked me up and down and back again, placing

and tracing my origin. All evening, they kept asking me
who made my dress *Who made your dress, dear?*

And to repeat my last name: *Knight* I said. *Knight*
as in black as the night sky above, everywhere stabbed

by blinking stars. Meaning: I come from the back
of the store, disheveled sale racks, everything 70% off,

marked down, price stricken through

with a giant red slash.

Conversation with Phillis Wheatley #14

recovered letter from Obour Tanner

To Phillis Wheatley in Boston [Massachusetts]

New Port, February 6th, 1772

Dear Sister,

I'm a savage. There is savage-me, inside, wild-thick as sin, so much, my Soul
is clabbered, but there is a Change, I sense, inside my curdled mess, Christ hung

and crucified in me, daily, a Saving Change. The ship. Do you feel the ship, pitching,
sometimes, inside the skin under your skin   -chanting-   as the Atlantic *whispered*,

lulling us, fluid as hymn and semen, in wet languages we couldn't understand?
                                                Remember the ships

that brought us over the bent world. Let us praise these wooden beasts that saved
the evil beast of us. Do you remember the ship, Phillis, do you remember rocking . . .

the rocking black milk, like I do? Remember the bowels from the reek
inside the deathly ship? There was nothing in us to recommend us to God,

except the bowels of divine love. Remember inky black, starless black,
blue-black with moaning, smelled like salt and salvation: God's skin hammered

with long nails like our breath, bleeding.

But we converted—we have been saved by a Saving
Change: my Heart is a true snow-white-snow Heart, of true Holiness, pure

as buttermilk, evangelical as buttermilk. But Repentance can save our people
from a land of seeming Darkness, and where the divine Light of revelation

(being cloaked) is as Darkness. What was darker than the bowels of that ship
you were named after, do you remember Phillis, how black, black is?

The mold? Our sin, the trigger—that mist was on everything, fuzzing our damp
little bodies with spores, encircling the air, emerald rust crawled and blossomed

inside our young lungs—it coughs and rackets the bright blood from us, like a claw
scraping, no, like soft applause from the balcony for the swarthy to sit upon

during church, like when me met, I was a dozen broken roses, bruised as velvet,
                                    English and reaching desire   for you,

across   the pews, across   the vast|empty spaces, where two slaves
    (who could read and write) could touch—each other—there, as women

and call it: Praise.

Let us marvel at the Love and Grace that bought

and brought us here.   Amen.

Your very humble servant and friend,

Obour Tanner

Ways to Be Saved

1. You are six and approached by a lady named Mabel. You think her name is maple syrup, as your skin and her skin are the color of pure sap. She leans down and grabs your cheeks with long, wetly glazed red apple acrylic fingernails. She asks—as if she herself is maple syrup being poured—*Do you love Jesus?* in a way that you will remember precisely for the rest of your life. You answer *Yes* because you'll give this sweet lady whatever she wants, but the question hovers, hummingbird flapping: the question, the name—Jesus, all of it, her full-bodied cinnamon-slick black hair drenched in Jheri curls dangling dew over your face, how she smelled like expensive bourbon—before you had the taste for dark liquor.

2. You are still a child when you walk down the altar and ask God to enter your little heart. You do not know what this means yet. An older man touches the top of your head. His white hand feels like a brick. You repeat after him. You repeat with all the other children chanting. You ask to be washed. You ask to be whiter than snow.

3. For the first time, you think about hell—a red devil poking fire at your feet until you dance—because you are ten years old and the children's pastor prays for you to receive the gift of tongues. The wet taste buds in your hands lift toward the metal faucet of heaven. Your fingers reach for a trickle of divine utterance, but there is no water for you. So you mimic: how they sway, close their eyes, wring their faces with a sweeter pain. You wonder why there is no angel on your shoulder whispering stretched out syllables on a loop. You wonder why your voice is not spun through a fan, reverberating.

4. You are in the backseat of a moving car. You are twelve. You want a kiss on the mouth, but he pushes your head down and makes you suck. You are thankful for the potholes on Old Hickory Boulevard that make the grill of your braces scrape the shaft of his penis. You get the taste for blood too early.

5. Solange.

6. Sixteen. A boy you are dating says he will give you your first orgasm. He moves his tongue the way you moved your tongue to speak to God as a child, except you still feel nothing. NOTHING. You pretend to give him what he wants. *God.*

7. Last year you wept/Listening to "Ultra Lightbeam" by Kanye West/You love Kanye West/ You think Kanye crazy/You think Kanye loves himself/Too much/You think Kanye thinks he's God/Or a god/Or maybe loving a black man/Or a self/Looks hard and divine enough/And it looks like this/Unhinged/Or maybe you think you have a little Kanye inside/Of you too/Tweeting ferociously inside of your chest/Humming/What looks like nonsense/What looks like he a baby/What looks like madness/To most/But you see/ You see the evidence of what faith looks like/Like/Outta the mouths of babes/Like Kanye loving himself/Like dying/Like dyeing his hair blonde/Or Blonde by Frank Ocean/Or Wesley Snipes in Demolition Man/You want the courage to love God like that—

8. A friend asks if you still go to church. You answer *no, but.* . . . You say this as a way to say *yes, and.* . . . Same as when you did improv—you be whatever your partner says you are. You become the thing and say: *yes, and.* . . . You follow the action by letting the scene develop through affirmation. You say this as a way to be saved.

9. You are a child again. You are waiting for your mom to come home. You are always waiting for your mom to come home. You are in a puddle of fake vomit made from Ranch and Thousand Island dressing. You have Band-Aids all over your body. You want to look like you are dead or dying. You are *As I Lay Dying*. But your mother is not a fish. You are the fish waiting to be eaten. Crucified. You practice at pain. You do this every day. Pretend. You make it look like you are hurt.

10. [   ]

Dead Bug

Ok, I said it.

I was twelve. I was in the backseat
of a moving car. I had a crush.
I was silent, except for my mouth

chock-full of braces and rape.
I've been writing around the rim
of the word like the blunted tip

of a spent bullet. But I said it.
I'm saying it now. I was twelve.
I was silent. I didn't stop it, ok.

I had a crush and the mind of a child.
When I was a [   ], I spoke as a
[   ], I understood as a [   ],

I thought as a [   ]: but when I became
[   ], I put away [   ] things.
I told you I had a crush. I'm telling you

I was crushed. I am crushing
the flood, overwhelming. What now?
There is a dead cockroach in the corner.

I won't pick it up. I keep sweeping
(around)
                the thing on the floor.

Tim

I don't know what happened   that night.
I was barefoot   sprinting   across a field of damp grass
and then I wasn't.   I was kissing a man—then I wasn't.
I was on a twin bed and then   and then . . . and then I was
blank—prone   on the dumb floor of a dorm room—
then I . . . I don't know   what happened to my panties.

Do you know what happened
to my panties?

Who took   them off—
Who entered   my body w/o asking—
Who saw   my cold nipples and said nothing—
Who saw   taupe watercoloring the rim
      of my eighteen-year-old breasts—
Who broke   my beaded black dress—
Who keeps the hours   I can't remember?

If faceless men came   into that room   then they have no names
and if I could scream   into that room   I'd shout: *Talitha kum!*
meaning   *Little girl,*   *I say to you, get up!*

28

~

Look deep inside the eye of a baby goat,
said Jessica, her command hung
at the back of the barn, lush imperative.

I gazed the animal eyeball, needling
the horizontal iris, its pupil so alien
from mine, a frazzled bleat cut

like the black bar inking the slit-shaped eye.
But there was another baby goat I called Tim
who was screaming at the seam of a corner

and when I approached   he ran away.
                I knew why.

~

Because   there are hours in my life
I cannot   remember
        that I don't want   to remember
                        and if I did

    I would have slaughtered Tim

and Tim smelled   this petite terror   on my hectic hands,
breath, and pits   spilling   black grease from my pores
like gasoline   slick,   savage with pheromones

and every time   I crunched one foot   closer
on the dank bed   of matted hay   and morning mud
to zip the space   between us   he kept leaping

and running,

                    breaking away

                                           from fear.

                    Tim, come here.

Dutchman in Reverse

after the play by Amiri Baraka

Take   the flesh   of chewed
          liquid   apple   put it back

in   the white   girl's   mouth
                                as firmament.
Take
          her knife, her   slick

tongue   and shut her up.

Take   the black man's body—

throw him   back   on the moving train.
Sit next   to him. Take her hand   off

his thigh.   Tell him
to keep reading.   Tell him

he is not hungry.   Tell him
he never   touched
his sister.

Tell him—   *Don't you dare*
          look out

that window.

800 Days: Libation

after not wanting to watch Time: The Kalief Browder Story *on Spike TV*

It rained inside me
it is raining inside my neck
the rain falls in sheets inside long sheets inside
all the rain is falling inside collapsing spit
I don't want to watch another black man die
today or know the story of how he died today
or how he was thrown away or how he ended up
I don't want to study the rain from inside
the house or overhear wild rain swell & thicken
slap the roof with wet words   & Kalief
who was there when you stopped
being & who was there when you were alone
& beyond yourself   how
the water around you from the island around you
might have sounded like a chorus   *who was there*
who was there   *who was there*   & now everyone
is watching your life from inside but I'm afraid to watch
them beat you   watch torture throbbing dry & long
with ache & blue-black bruising   so I don't
& another black body is blown out   smoking wick
the lone wisp of a life lingers smelling burnt & gone
how rain wraps round a tornado is a type of sorrow
because no one knows how to fathom damage inside
someone's eyes could be the weather just after or before
a storm   calm & clear but still bleaker inside the black
parts of the pupils the holes smooth black holes in the eyes
as they left you in the hole with no rain   & I'm emptying
a waterfall shouting   KALIEF

I want you to be undead & not alone   lonely in the ground
again   I want I want (the "I" wants so much) how it greeds
like a fist   of pounding rain on your body bleating broke
but what I want doesn't matter what I want are rare blossoms
for the dead   because you're gone & your mother is gone
all because someone said you stole a backpack meaning
your body was made a forgotten altar your body made bodiless
kept pushing back as your trial kept pushing back & back &
black matter moves backwards in time meaning   Kalief matters
in the past tense even though the space around your life didn't
matter to them   or them   or them   like the space that scatters
& navigates around the circumference of raindrops is never wet
& the braided distance between you & me   is dry & long
like time is rainless with a tight & loaded lungful blowing 800
candles out for the 800 days in solitary your brain behind bars
fades your body in confinement your chest caged alone
your body alone all   I   hear   is your name falling
& beating *Kalief*   *Kalief*   *Kalief Kalief Kalief*
this is such a poor offering but I am pouring it on the ground
like good rain & whatever softens the earth is your name
whatever might grow from that darkening bright spot is your name
lapping little lakes of creation turning mud in your name
whatever might be fed from the liquid raining inside me
whatever might be loosened from the muck & the dark
rum pouring from my bottle   & Kalief   your name   is drizzling
a type of grief upon my mouth like mist as it reigns
inside me it is raining inside my body the rain falls in sheets
inside all the rain is untangled & not touching
who touched you with tenderness falling inside

& Kalief
what is there to say
after so much rain

the ground is swollen with your name

The Ayes Have It

When I think of Trayvon Martin, I think of Emmett Till,
        when I think of Emmett Till, I think of young, black men in the South,

then I think of young, white men in the South.
        I think of my husband, who is white, born and raised in Franklin, TN.

I think of how when he tries to hold my hand,
        sometimes I pull away and not because I don't love him,

but because I'm alert, I think of other people,
        other people who are born in the South,

that remember the Old South and in fact long for it.
        I think about the nooses that hung on our back porch

when I was little: one for me and one for my mom,
        I think about how people say

It's not about race, don't make it about race,
        I wish black people would stop talking about race!

When all I've ever known is being defined by my race.
        What are you? Where are you from?

I say *California*, but that's not what they are looking for—
        they are asking about my parents.

What they want to know is that my mother is black
        and my dad is white. *I'm mixed.*

So when I think about a post-racial America, I don't—
        because the trees in the South have strange fruit histories,

the roots are deep red, tangled and gnarled, so again—
        when I think of Trayvon, I think of hoodies, then I think

of stereotypes, I think of skittles and high fructose corn syrup,
        tasting the rainbow, and then I think of gay marriage,

then just marriage in general and then I'm back to my husband,
        and see he's trying to hold my hand again, but the truth is I'm scared,

because I have to love him differently in the South,
        just like young, black men have to exist differently in the South,

they can't just wink at any woman, Mr. Till,
        just walk through any neighborhood, Mr. Martin,

just wear any hoodie, buy any iced tea. Someone is watching,
        always watching us, so when I think about justice,

I think about eyeballs, the first impression,
        the action that follows, George Zimmerman stepping

out of his car. I think what would have happened
        if he'd just given him a ride home?

Ode to the *Only Living Object that Survived*

after the volcanic eruption of Mount Pelée
on May 8, 1902, which killed over 30,000 people.

Praise Mount Pelée: the eruption. Praise pyroclastic flow. Praise

Ludger Sylbaris and his stone cell that saved him from the volcano.

Praise the murder? That placed him inside the cleft of a mountain, alone

with only a tiny window to the apocalyptic world. Praise

his quick wit with urine soaked clothes sucking smoke. Praise

dreadful burns on his back like frozen black lava. Praise

lava roiling in the rocky veins of the earth like blood rivers, crazy and scorching. Praise

Barnum and Bailey Circus for displaying this man around the world. Praise

the billboard: *Only living object that survived in the 'Silent City of Death.'* Praise

the duplicate of his prison for the show. The handbill read:

Most Marvelous Man in the World. Praise

how to sell a *thing*, a burned object. Praise

circus marketing. Keep praising

the circus for its beautiful freaks of our broken nature. Praise

the circus, I say. Praise

the circus for the first black man to star

in the segregated show, The Greatest Show on Earth. Praise

the object, 1) something visible or tangible 2) focus 3) goal. Praise

the noun affected by the verb and the KELOIDS—agate and smooth

on his skin 7) source of light rays. Praise

the punching verb and the noun and the man/and the man/and the man

who survived the end of his world. All his people are gone, praise!

To be saved, for what? This. Me? Making him an object, again—objectified ode, again

becoming a *thing*, glossy with advertising. I can see him so clearly, looking back at me

through bars and then becoming the bars and then becoming the world before me

like light. Praise his testimony. Praise

the witness and his blistered onyx back, cracked coal, black tephra. Praise

pryoclast: meaning fire + *broken in places*. Praise

a man without a city, his people: scorched and suffocated

from insidious gas or the searing belch of reckless lava. Praise

him on display, a lit and exotic tableau. Praise

the stage

name. Praise

the engine of his story rattled again and again like a fiction, a lie that dazzles

into a safer display. A safer spectacle: of otherness. Praise:

Cain-cursed with magical crust, armored melatonin. Praise

his real name: August. Behold him stepping into his nightly prison. Praise

him—his own costume inside another costume, himself leathered skin,

himself praise enough, to endure and keep enduring eyeballs. Praise

production: fake bars closing—fake smoke misting/rising/and misting.

Now cue the drums mimicking volcano shivers, the drums undulating

the hem of the tent, quaking the little atmosphere. Praise

the barker booming about wonder, the white *WONDER of it ALL*! Praise

the people aghast at his survival and scarred skin, all diamanté and post-lava.

I want to go there now, because again, I can see him so clearly.

I want to watch the show—as he watches me—watch him, to look through him

till he becomes the start of me, a freakish place of praise like in the zoo

with Rilke's panther pacing & passing what seemed like a thousand bars.

The man has become his cage—has become a mountain within a mountain

about to burst with liquid fire. Now, he: the month of August with all its tortured, trapped heat. Praise

the miraculous object—like a doll—I want to pluck

him from the billowing tent with my god fingers;

                              snuff out the tent

                                        with my god fist.

II. ABOUT THE TREES

And I won't tell you where it is, so why do I tell you
anything? Because you still listen, because in times
like these to have you listen at all, it's necessary
to talk about trees.

                                ↁ *Adrienne Rich*

After *Apollo*

pas de deux with Terpsichore,
choreographed by George Balanchine, 1928

Their flexed index fingers   delicately   click
and breathe together—   the fluid dance begins

as if God and Adam   are closing in—

There is so much delightful prosody,   all white
in the middle   of her lustrous, muscled   legs

swaying   over the golden head   of God.
Three times   Apollo takes her petite wrist, dips

her down   toward the smooth and continuous
earth   spilling the muse   like a porcelain cup

pouring more cream   on cream
backgrounded by a stage of Prussian blue: steely

arrows inside   the storm-colored eyes of Apollo.
This god lifts her again   over his clavicle   and she

is draped   against his back   like warm bath water
poured over and streaming down   the knotted spine

as Stravinsky's strings   stretch   and vibrate—
the wooden cavity   of taut instruments.

How the dancers make   a frothy   waterfall
of each other's Caucasian   bodies,   all adagio

Calliope, Polyhymnia, and Balanchine   are offstage.
No one is talking here—   Apollo was just born

and now   she is rearing the child   inside of him.
With her back to me   she sits on the trunk

of his legs   and offers him   her liquid gifts
through the wet   and taut positions   of ballet,

shows him   how she splits   herself
(as I have)   again   and again

for such a   gorgeous,   foolish God
                                        and man.

After *Agon*

pas de deux featuring Arthur Mitchell & Diana Adams, the first interracial duet
in American ballet, choreographed by George Balanchine, 1957

A battle of skin   movement   through   & under
& perpendicular. . . .   I want   your forearm   on my   forearm
like   that.   White woman :: Black Man in constant   cruciform,

duet: touch her ankles as if thick lilies   grow there,   pluck
                                      her wrist as if it is your wrist there.

Are you the caregiver or patient? What sickness can I fondle that isn't already
inside me too? Can you hold the body on point   //as if to cut//   the invisible
knife between us—atoms splitting themselves   biracial:

one & two/& one & two/&   what are you?   Insert: skin tone/atonal.

Cradle my torso: teach me to walk   again. Tanaquil Le Clercq, Ballachine's
wife lost her fawn legs to polio. Diana's able body is her body now, but muses
don't need to strut → to run → to be. This music is-is-is-is-is making me anxious.

That's it: stop & start again, between breathing, soft iron   lung.
Staccato à la Stravinsky!   Insert: inhale/exhale.

Arthur is all aplomb. Arthur is what black is {muscular and agog}. Diana's leg
alabaster in arabesque → above Arthur's head. Her leg, a needle through the eye
of him. Her leg, a slow hour hand in silk pantyhose alight on Arthur's clavicle,

physical clock, the intricate machine: 1 & zero/& 1 & zero/& . . .

Arthur, move the white woman there   and there   now here.   Diatonic &
clumsy violin chords pull frenetic. She   cannot move   without   you
tending to her limbs. She cannot   move without   you   glazing   her stretch

and splay—

her far-reaching, frosted legs bend & slice, little angles lush   with geometry.
one & two/& one & two/& three & four/& five & sex—6. I mean 6!   Ahhhh,
so much fear that is & is not here. The audience watches the fight   adagio:

tangle & unweave/weave & untangle. Whatever struggle is in my skin   let it
dance   upon my mulatto body   to make my thighs twist
                                                                                & weep.

Oh Arthur, what is Mr. B telling me here? I've been staring at the only picture
of my dad. He is holding my mom at her hips. I am trying to find what   parts
of me   are his.

She is smiling & he is smiling, but he does not show   his teeth.

After *Orpheus*

pas de deux with Eurydice,
choreographed by George Balanchine, 1948

The son of Apollo   has no voice   here—
only the music   of Stravinsky's symphony.
The dancers sing   with their unbolted bodies,

wholly lengthened   and   phantasmagoric.
The Dark Angel leads   him through the lyre,
through unfolding   underworld—his hand:

another type of lung, breathing.   Balanchine
wanted the audience to see each finger   splayed
and reaching,   extended. But when   the anxious

Orpheus tears off his mask, the ballerina   collapses
for the floor. The curtain billows   and the oboes
are gone. I think about patience   and its stupid song.

I can't wait—   Yes, I'm always looking   back

                    at my dead.

What the ghost wants

is not always
obvious—

~ *Kevin Young*

The Rime of Nina Simone

Argument

*How a Slave Ship was driven by capitalism and racism inside the triangle
of the transatlantic slave trade; and of the strange things that befell;
and in what manner Nina Simone came back from the dead to her
own Country to stop a graduate student on the way to workshop.*

~

I didn't recognize her at first,
but felt urgency inside her glittering
eyes—grotesque and morganite,
melting blooms. Her skin, stabbed

with hammered copper, afro nimbus,
the luminous gaze, an X-ray swishing
at my skin with metronomic waves.
Timeworn but regal, her spine

made of satin and salt, her bolted
black back clutching every battle-born
ballad: a lone column of glissandos
and thunder snow, booming and bright.

Come here, she says.

Sorry, I can't—I'm late. I'm—

I need to tell you something   about yourself.

Listen, little girl:

For every pain
there is a longer   song.

     The body pours

                     its own music.

        I wanted
        to play Bach
        and Beethoven
        for endless encores. But

they wouldn't let me
and they won't let you.

Things have changed, Miss Simone.
I have a scholarship. They want me here.
They want my poems. They want—

        Do they want you,
        she says, sucking
        her ghost teeth,
        or your black pain?

What's the difference? I say.

        Ha, does your mother know what you write?

Yes, but not the mother poems.

She grabs my shoulders, slides her shivering hands
down my stiff arms. She's holding me like an auntie—
I soften and she's got me and I'm hers.

                Nina begins:

                During revivals, syrup would fly
                from every black-boned believer,
                releasing righteous temper.
                The Holy Roller Ghost
                caught me young—
                blew my sails southward
                to quiver at the touch   of Jesus. Jesus,
                we'd shout on refrain—shred
                and siphon maple from marrow,
                silver spiles biting delicious bark
                            tapping   fluid sugar
                and red kino from our rough-hewn throats
                every Sunday morning
                for the first service
                then for choir practice
                at 3 and 6 P.M. and Wednesday night
                for prayer meeting and Friday night
                for choir practice again and again drizzling the pews
                            with pure delight and little me
                            at the piano sweeping up all that sway
                          all that fantastic black energy
                          from the preacher and the congregation.

It was a white lady, Miz Mazzy,
who taught me to sit and play correctly
at the piano—use the oil
in my shoulders   not my wrists.

Eight hours a day
until the ivory keys and my pirouetting
fingers became one gigantic song,
          a symbiosis. Symphonies
          like burning white lye—saponified
          with my skin.
I stopped reading
sheet music and closed
my eyes to lidded
          charcoal—

          felt the night
                    ocean stirring beneath roused
                    from the furthest habitations
                    of my blood
as my wavering body
became a front porch
row of rocking
          chairs facing east—always
          east toward France,
                    before I even knew
I wanted freedom
from   freedom.

Felt glacial depths—   wet and coffinless:
         transatlantic moan,   simmer
         and hiss, beautiful   sharks
inside me: water boiled
into black mist
              cumulus   clouding into songs
                          of resistance hovering
                          above the slaver's pitching, slippery deck
                          (easier access to the wenches pinned
                          in steel cages—gripped hands lacquered
                          like abacus beads on bars),

different tongues mosaic with Gold, Ivory, and Pepper coast melodies
                              cradling   starless nights.

Every time I loomed   the deep
I became another person.

The body   is a ship
constantly cutting   lathering water
in the way ships
              yearn

for imagined shores, bobbing
in the immediate distances.

                   My low contralto rasping   in the offing
                   chased   the dipping prow

above the moon-drenched water,   rippling
        with magnificent milk and midnight
        plashing. I sailed the white froth

of my suffering   until everything bled
        clear, till there was nothing in my mouth
        but the wounded side   of Jesus
                where they knifed him,
                        till there was nothing
                        but loose gravel, diminishing
                        applause . . .

What about your missing teeth? I ask, as I attempt to touch her face,
her cheek, her skin shifting into a wooden artist palette, gauzy and dripping
dreamlike, oil-thick paint smearing pinks and reds and browns with knives—
carnations for eyes. I reach inside her cave-cool mouth for broken keys
and the 22nd century. Cabernet bruises on her lovely-love head and lips.

        Punches from my albatross   hung

        around my neck, she says.

I shot the thing that was hurting me:
                                my husband
                                (*who brought the fog and mist*).

Slime-green with my money
and decay.
                    Dead necklace.

I was carrying
                    the dead load
                    of his animal stench:

oh how he loved
to work me like a dray
horse   and I bucked

until I adored his sable fist more than the sex
or the furs in cold storage   or the baby's little fingers reaching,
reaching for my pearls   or the yellow pills to keep me singing
and galloping   across the glistering globe.

The whip has always
                    made the body
                              dance and crack.

        I jerked and wailed, spasmodic.   Me, the black spider

damned by angry gods and angry hands   in the hands
                    of an angry God!   I dangled
                                                          over wildfire.

The art of tamping—espresso—folding dark meadows inside
my throat: fluttering uvula, lone pink hibiscus in praise.

                                        I unbuckled my trauma
                                        one note at a time.

                One note at a time
                                        I un-buck-led
                                        my trauma.

Woke up
drenched in cold sweat
and furiously
tried to remember
my only dream:
                                        FINALLY

playing a Bach
cantata at Carnegie Hall

                                        FINALLY
the audience would
shut up and listen

in the way
I needed them to listen   to me.

All   quiet
as fresh snow muffling
early morning trees,
a hushing frost
on the meadow sparkling
with untracked fondant.

But it never happened. They only
wanted cocktail jazz, folk, and blues,

for me to bleed negro, a signifyin(g)
monkey from my classical piano.

They only wanted that Swing low,
Sweet chariot strain, but I smashed it all

together anyway, making and breaking
forms on the bridge between my voice

and finger play. My vinyl sorrow spinning,
spinning the grind against cuspate needle.

My records swarthy as the beloved skin
of Cain, bitten. I silenced the audience

with one   long   glare.

She pauses to show me her famous Midtown stare.

Like a ghost ship, I wandered from stages to states
and countries and colleges, concert after concert.

I unglued
        myself
        in hotel mirrors
        until I disappeared
        visions of laser beams
        and skin, always skin
        sliced with heaven,
        lingering scent
        of a burnt-out
        bulb—still,
        incandescent,
        the weirdness.

They said my blue note
baritone could find the tiniest sack
                        of unsent tears   inside
                        anybody. Any   body.

Called me Black Bitch: Diva. Demanding. Difficult.
Depressed. Genius. Monster.

They don't call me that here. *Well, not to my face.*
I can write about anything I want. *I think.* Here . . .

here are the dead bodies and bullets in my work.
Here are the four little girls, I say as I hold up my poems.

Look, if you can write about anything   you want,
    Then write. About. Anything.   *You* want.
    Why do you keep panting & hunting   black hurt,
    black scars like a slave-breaker?   Why scratch
    the white page, a master,   for old blood?
    Like a god, you are   so thirsty,
    hell-bent on carving beauty   from dead bodies
    from sacrifice   on the altar.

Because

I listen to the trees
humming through the poplar leaves

and Southern magnolias. Bloated faces,
these beauteous forms, still swinging,

limp pendulum, waxy bleach-white blooms,
egg whites inside hardboiled eyes

sway and rock, roll forward, fragrant.
I'm ready to find the ruined churches.

(In hours of weariness, sensations sweet,
felt in the blood, and felt along the heart.)

I have a second stomach now. Now
I can look at my dead   and listen.

Listen, I'm transcribing the soaked,
splattered leaves—

                    You sound so tired, my darling . . .
                                             You weary yet?
                    she whispers in my ear, of creating and fighting . . .
                    can you stay a dog chained
                    barking at every threat, out of breath
                    in the darkness—and the darkness
                    is always you—panting for more food
                    to get published, for what? This?

Yes. This:
I need to be here—in the workshop.
I must look them in the face
and tell them when their words
and worlds are making me uncomfortable.

Tell them when my chest tightens and flares up
when they try to conjure the other, a fantastic
field of fictitious black and brown bodies.

Tell them my body is real—not imagined,
not a prop or sieve or a literary device.
Not foil. Not craft. Not carnal. Not chocolate.
Not mammy or mask or persona. Not opposite
of the white gaze. I must tell them that my:

lips/butt/haircurlers are mine/urban/slang/long
fingernails/arrested/dialectic are mine/burning/
erotic hottentot/blue bandanna/Beyoncé/like-like
liquor/blasting the classroom with my noisy stereo-
types, shouting: I. Am. Here. You cannot write
around me. The periphery is also mine. I'm not
afraid to take up the space I need to survive.
I'm not afraid to write what I need to survive.

> Mmmmm . . . write what *you* need, ha!
> Be careful now. They might snatch that money back real quick
> > when you start talking revolutionary—
> > what's your compulsion?

The Slave Ship :: war machine.
Robert Hayden's *Jesus   Saviour   Pilot   Me.*

I can't talk about the trees
without the blood.

> *Baby, you can't put a fire out—*
> > *or fold a flood . . .*

> Didn't Emily D. say that? Didn't you learn?

> *A Thing that can ignite*
> *Can go, itself, without a Fan—*
> *Upon the slowest Night—*

> Why are you still afraid to say *goddamn*?

Feels wrong
like I'm sinning
like God can't see my face.
I know I'm not sinning,
leftover fear from church,
makes my sternum lead
heavy, 'bout to break—

       Then you are not ready!
       It's not enough for you to be young,
       gifted, black   and angry

       or write a few poems about *the body.*
       The body. The body. The body . . .
       she says, mocking me with her hands,

       then points her diaphanous finger in my face—

       You have to stay mad
                  your whole damn life.

       You have to make love
       to the damage
       in your mind—return
           to the throbbing meadow
       you know will pang

when you enter the middle
                              of its wild scrape.

Pick up your stone. Find water.
                    Just let it skip, baby,
let it skip—like birth,
all this pushing, all this labor
leads to life.

Has a man ever hit you?

No

            Have you ever wanted a man to hit you?

Yes

        Why?

I wanted to feel as bruised
as you did on the inside, something cellular
like begging on my knees, because . . .
it was still someone touching me
besides myself. Because fathers. Because
poems are part animal + part pain machine
tearing at flesh, holy somatic control, I guess.

And in that brief moment
before climaxing

when I choose to release
my thighs inside
another aching vessel
in that slick, dark, dank slave ship heat—
and in that moment right after
they come (when I dislike myself the most)—
that's when I want to be punched
with how lonely I am.

      Pfft. What the hell is your maiden name? she says.

Knight

      Why did you change it?

Thought I was supposed to—
wanted to be married so damn bad
that I . . . I didn't think about saving my name.

But I heard the snipping,
bifurcation from black women
in my family, ripping

and weeding me
from the soil
and scion of single mothers

on their knees,
chalked with ash
interceding for me.

A curse. My mother
would say and pray away
till she walked me down

the aisle to a white man:
from a good family
on the good side of town

with good credit.

You like those white boys, don't you?

Yes

Why?

I'm attracted to things
that once owned me.
I'm attracted to men
who don't want me,
men who give me their seed
and disappear
when I am born again
and again and
again and—

She saunters
back to her grave
        humming something familiar
        I cannot name.

I almost catch the hem of her song,
but it slips as she slips away.

I walk to class. My spine, a grounded stake
lit with liquid brass and burning peaches.

Bewitched—ready to flame: I enter the room—

                                      bursting.

III. WITHOUT THE BLOOD

When I passed by you and saw you squirming in your blood,
I said to you while you were in your blood, 'Live!' Yes, I said
to you while you were in your blood, 'Live!'

⌇ Ezekiel 16:6–7

BBHMM

after watching the music video

I, too, want to be naked,   zebra-striped
in the almost dried accountant's blood,   sticky
and sucking   a fat blunt inside a Louis Vuitton
suitcase brimming   with the newest money.

This   is another way to see myself, too,
in the way Rihanna   nooses   a white woman   up
by her smooth feet, a blue-blooded pendulum   swaying
as her beautiful tits   look more perfect than ever.

Why did that image excite me so?   No,   not the tits,
but the simulated lynching.   It feels so damn
delicious   to say bitch.   *Bitch better/bitch better have*
my money inside my mouth.   I hate it when people

talk about black artists   being capitalists.
Why can't we thrive in something rich and green too? And let us
be loud about it? Let us be loud   without consequence.
Remember, when we were dating? I wanted you   to pay

for every meal, and yes, the movies taught me that love
was someone reaching for the check   first.
But *there is no such thing as a free lunch*. Someone
has to pay   with the fruit from their body.   Yeah, I'm spreading

my legs   for someone else, because I'm hungry   and always
at the end of some kind of altar.   Even now, I'm paying   for my doctor

to reach and scrape inside me   to say   I don't have cancer.
She tells me   I need to start thinking about babies

because of my age.   I think, *Bitch* . . .   I'm not ready.
There will always   be tithes and offerings. At my church,
they called it *first fruits*.   My mother gave me quarters
and as a kid   I waited for the clink at the bottom

of the bucket being passed. I believed God heard this too.
Somewhere   someone is counting the cash behind a velvet curtain.
Once, a boy said, *suck it, bitch*   with his heavy, dense hand
at the back of my head   pushing. Pushing   is

another way to mean   *pay me what you owe me*. I didn't forget.
Yeah, I see the total   at the bottom of the receipt.
I have so much   debt.
                         I am forever   in the wettest red.

First Tree, at Church Camp

We felt naughty—so we climbed
the big magnolia behind the church.
Genesis, Exodus, Leviticus, Numbers . . .
We loudly intoned the books of the bible
like a spell or counter spell to bless
and curse the whole burnt summer
with me and the white boys,
me surviving the white boys,
only black girl dense with city, urbanized
and now my first tree, every branch coarse
with nature—scratchy bark chalked
my shins with ash. It did not matter.
I was a dauntless ten-year-old.
My hands daubed with thick sap as I groped
for ascension limb after limb, leading the boys.
Air dense with our grunting and taunting hymns
of who could get to the top first, the five of us
dotted around the wooden crinoline.

I told the boys I had to pee. The boys said
I could pee in the tree just like them,
and showed me their golden parabolas shooting
from their centers in a single, continuous stream.
It was such a beautiful dare. Thinking
I was no different, I pulled down my shorts
and tried. I did not squat. I could be a fountain
just like them if my body would engender me so.

I had fresh hope for my liquids, but I just pissed
all over myself, warm rivulets down my legs,
my pink socks and shoes, my khaki shorts,
and a little puddle inside my panties wrapped
around my ankles. Laughter erupted
from the white boys—their happiness even stronger
outside of their dry bodies, inside their convenient
penises. Smell of me yellowed with salt, shamed.

The gospels became brassier and endless: *Matthew,*
Mark, Luke, John . . . Matthew, Mark, Luke, John . . .
as my wondrous glory glistened. I covered myself,
slinked down the rough trunk in defeat, squished and raw.
I threw away my socks and sat in the Tennessee heat
alone—thinking how my body was different, so fearfully
and wonderfully made different.

After that, I didn't play with the white boys anymore.

It did not matter.
I would soon be all woman.
I would soon know about the blood.

First Blood

I'd been praying
between my legs
to become all woman
& know about woman things
like sex & Mother said
she would tell me
once I started with the blood
& from my new lower body
I wrung with fresh heat
confused why women
bled at their centers
& Mother began
with the hymen
said the man with his knife-
like penis pierces
the fleshy wall inside
the vagina shredding
& the woman bleeds
but in a *different way*
this time
there are so many ways
to become a woman
so many ways
a body injures & leaks
with knowledge
everything bleeds
so terribly
I don't blame her now

for my present hesitations
but I'm not ready
to confront that corner
in the waiting room
of my lower body
so let's go back
to the yelling
I remember yelling
I will never have sex
I will never have sex
& she was so pleased
by my screams
I crossed my legs
to close my cramping
& future fears
& we were silent again
with all this new
knowledge between us
with the red wild
& wider between us

Self-Portrait as First Kiss

My braces cut you—
metallic scythe,

nicking your bottom
fat lip into another

ruby mouth drawing
caterpillar blood

three beads dripped,
spilling a tiny river—

liquid dahlias
and burning raspberries

on some stove. I felt
your tongue—a pink

dolphin arcing the pink
muscle in my mouth

to undulate. Years later,
I would see your cherubic,

white face, this time lit
inside a box—frozen

bright from a mug shot
on the news, wanted

by the police for kid-
napping and torturing

a black woman. A black
woman you thought stole

the drug money hidden
inside the cotton lips

of your mattress and bed
frame. They said you tied

her to a chair and I won't
say what you did next. It's

too unbearable to say here—
inside a couplet that can't

stop the shattering glass
you broke inside of her.

I won't say what you said
to me—after I made you

bleed, opened you rare
as a new wound. I won't

talk about the scar
I scraped into the velvet

puckering of your lip
or how you called it

your *love nick*—looked
like a thin piano key

that you once tapped,
a sharp note begging

with your index finger
and I kissed you again

because I felt bad
for cutting you in this way.

It takes a special kind
of cruelty to damage another.

Lil' Chris, do your lips still
itch for me or the dope,

knocking and unknocking
your mouth for more

and more blood?

What the Blood Does

ending with a line from Mark 8:24

Inside   the sanctuary

of my gelatinous   brain

every moment   thwacks against itself

massive   amounts of water   slapping

millimeters   off crags—   a lynching

picture slips   under a lake like silt,   twirling, deciding

some miracles take time,   perhaps, in two steps:

I see trees, but they look like men,   hanging.

I see men, but they look like trees,   *walking*

               (on fire).

Where the Fired Body Is Porous

The Smell of Me—
is on his pillow, scent
                    of unwrapped hair,
slick perfume
with grease and caged fumes.

From the morning:
of sizzling ceramic blades—pressing heat
and circadian fire on my 3C black curls,
after-singe of straightening (white boy
sniffing me for kindling).
Signature of black char. We are tangled
in the womb of his dorm room.

It is the first time—

His roommate's neon sign:
a blond and busty St. Pauli girl hovers
on the wall behind my head.

                    Corona of hot blue sky condensation
                    as her white savior arms spread
                    in crucifix, offering foam-covered heads
                    of electric beer spilling and buzzing thin, a little hum
                    like a fat bee caught in a neon blue bug zapper—

                                        continuous stinging,
voltaic and numinous flushing
glazed white cinderblocks, cold
to the touch of my clammy hand
with shadows glowing gauze
and chiffon—navy smearing
to gray silk—early dusk: the body knowing
how and when to absorb another.

My hair smoldering like lit patchouli
                as my weather-beaten strands swirl
                on his white pillow—sweat collecting
                at my edges, moisture and dirt churning loam.

Because I want my smell brackish
and full of darker climates,
I do not wash my hair every day.

Yes, full of thunderstorm
and terracotta, baked earth and spangled with Tennessee pollen.
From the bar the night before, from
                bummed Marlboro Reds
                                        and the bonfire plume
                                                (the week before that)
                a drizzle of embers cooling and falling to white ash,
                sticking to my hair like dirty snowflakes

for nine days—hermetic in my glory. My dust all pressing,
pressing into his white pillow like a sponge—porous
as he presses into me—stirring the soil, alluvial.

Fingernails dig into my scalp, muddy with my dark
dandruff. Raking through knotted black wool, curling thick
at the root as I steep, decide to lose my body.

My hair spools the blood,   another helix
                                                                              /rich

with description.

He is reaching for my kitchen.

                              Unruly secret at the nape of my neck.
Hush now—
: All those gleaming pots and pans.
: All those cabinets I keep shut.   Hush.
                                             I am undone and open.
No order is here/can't find nuthin' back there/except
a little me/in a chair by the stove:
              hot comb on the black burner, another red tornado.
              Mama standing,
              bowing my head downward—bending me
                                             into a black comma.
                                      Pressing my hair—smooth.
              Holding back my ears as I hold back my breath.
Gettin' cooked. Always afraid Mama
                                             would burn me.
But—   I am clanging, full
of kinks,
teeming with my own spice: turmeric, clove, paprika—
grains of paradise   liquid/smoke.

Self-Portrait as Hannah Peace

at the Cotton Eyed Joe in Knoxville, TN,
adapted lines from Sula *by Toni Morrison*

Mamma, did you ever love me?   I whisper the words   to myself,
watching her line-dancing in a western bar   to a country song

                                                     Hannah burning

about beer and horses   and ripped denim   as woozy spotlights
cascade   around her body.   *I mean, did you? You know.*

                                                     the flames

When I was little   hold me   the way mothers hold the whole
of their children   trying to get them back inside their bodies,

                                                  from the yard fire

rock me   against the fever   of your own warmth, watch me sleep,
count   my baby breath   against the heft of your own. She beckons

                                                    licking

me to dance with her,   but I do not come to the only black person
scuffing up the hardwood floor.   I wish I could swivel my body

                                                    the blue

next to her two-stepping feet,   fumble to keep count, the turns and kicks,
but I do not come. She becomes   another woman on the dance floor,

                                                    cotton dress

a happier woman   I do not recognize   and she keeps begging me,
slow-motioning her forearms: little shadowy waves   lapping

                                                    making her dance

under frantic disco lights.   All.   You want me.   To do.   Is dance.
But I leave her alone,   her rusted red cowboy boots turning, turning

                                                    Hannah burning

to music I do not like.   *Awww, Mamma,* remember the Christmas
with no presents?   You said it was going to be real lean   that year—

                                                    I was thrilled

that year I stayed in my room,   read and read, shifted my shoulders
from one side of the bed to the other,   another type of dancing,

I wanted her

dancing as I turned each page and wept. You fell asleep on the couch
that night too.   But *Mamma*, remember   the next Christmas?

to keep on jerking

That year you wrapped each individual crayon,   made it look like more.
That year you signed every gift   from: *Santa Mamma.*

like that

You wanted me to know   it came from you and your three jobs
and not some white man.   You did things like that, *Mamma.*

and yet

I know you fed me   *and all* those payments for my braces.
But I let my teeth turn back, crooked.   I'm sorry.

Hannah burning

But *did you ever . . . you know, play with me*   before I stopped
wanting   to play with you?   I don't sing or dance

Hannah burning

on command   for you anymore—   *Ain't that love?*
Or something like it . . .   a daughter watching her mother dance.

Ain't that love?

Mother Driving Away After Christmas

She hobbles to her car on crunchy knees
into vague mist after a wash of thunderstorms.

I wait for her ignition in the way she must
have waited for my first damp breath and fuzz

of lanugo sweeping her cinnamon cheek.
She drives to her city—two hours from mine,

no one there to greet her. She drives the concrete
purr of interstate as a carol whimpers out.

She is alone, and yet, not alone. Other cars
swim around her silence like plump, metal fish

zooming through the drowsy night. Mother,
let the glint of street lights flick, let my prayers

watch over you now. Her hands gripping tighter
on the warm steering wheel—been holding firm

her whole life, except for when she walked me
down the aisle, her hands were open and mush then.

She drives away from me into the stirring dark
tank I once knew inside of her, when I was just

diaphanous, a cluster of fluffy chromosomes,
singing flotsam in her glowing pregnant belly—

her one good thing inside this hurt, traveling home.

In the Middle of Things . . .

written during a lecture about narrative opacity

My daddy   is what   is always   at stake   in my work.
I want to know if he is still   alive—
if he thinks of me as often as I think of him.

I am still that baby, alone
in the incubator, yelping   for more and more breath
with moist, moth-like wings for lungs.

Only my mother's name is on my birth certificate.
Her hand pausing   or maybe
                                        it was more like hovering.
Her hand   leaving something blank for me.

This is the restless cardboard box   I carry from room to room, house to house
filled with papers I do not know   how to sort. How do you separate trash
        from trash? Everything looks like something else—something
I just might need. Someday, right?

I do not know where to put my father: the idea of him
or just his hands?   (I imagine them calloused, muddy inside the fingernails)
I find him asleep, in my dreams, stare at the beads dancing under his eyelids,
twitching as if in code, little familiar movements. Maybe he is dreaming

of my coarse, horse-like hair   as I am of his. Maybe   we both wake
in the media res of midnight and say each other's names, except   I'm not sure
if he knows mine. Maybe he simply whispers   *Somewhere I have a little girl*
to the dumb   always-listening dark cloud above our beds,

that constant black static   never answers
but records our dim desires for anyone to touch us—   touch us
where we were never touched   by our fathers,
which for me → would be everywhere: on my skin, caramelized,

left to be burned and sugared,   every inch of me
without his scent or marking, except   on my left butt cheek,
you see, I have his birthmark there.   *You have his birthmark there*,
my mother says and says, *Same spot!*   Is this how you absorb the life

of a missing person . . .   through a freckled, milk-coffee spot?
Who cares about another bastard? Who cares about his skateboard?   I do.
His hair thick and lacquered and damp as a bowl of pitted black olives,
the sheen of which could make you weep   if you lingered there.

But I choose your name, Augustine. Your name   every night
when my man reaches for the fog   between my breasts. I dream—
I dream you are reaching for me   saying what . . .   I still cannot see.

Freelove in Retrograde

She asks the boy—*Is it cloudy or clear*?
He mews half asleep in the bluing drag of dawn.
My great-grandmother glares through ten miles

to Miss Austin's house, but the house is gone.
No wet laundry to wring and clean but her own.
In the corner lies her battered Bible and shotgun.

Autumnal wind whistles fierce through the shotgun
house. Great-grandmother looks through the clearing
to find the tall fescue path she walked and owned.

North Carolina breaks the navy back of night over dawn.
She is alone, except for the boy. The family has gone
to war, fighting in Negro battalions, so many miles

from home. Miles from Warrior—miles from miles,
the distances milked from her twelve-gauge shotgun,
blasted drunk Uncle Leroi in the foot, pinky toe gone.

She asks the waking boy again—*Is it cloudy or clear,
boy*? But. The answer doesn't matter anymore. Dawn
cracks the glistening frost on drying tobacco, to own

a simple thing: the used Maytag machine she now owns.
If it rained that day—she didn't have to walk for miles
to Miss Austin's house to clean her soiled clothes, dawn-

ing pickled fingers against a washboard—pain like a shot
gunning through her palms. Her hands huge inside clear
water, now on the boy's back jostling him awake—gone

is the rain. She knows the answer, still wants the boy gone—
to walk out the door and testify if the day is for their own.
He emerges from cool sheets, makes the bed, clearing

dreams of his dead mother from his head. Warrior is miles
from nothing, pinned under Black Mountain's shotgun
tip. Blue Ridge blankets the state in sheets of restless dawn.

In the beginning she reads from Genesis. How the dawn
of man came from good dirt. The dirt road now gone
and paved. Now, I want the gun. *Who has her shotgun?*

Her black finger on the trigger, Freelove holds her own
without a man for provision, holds the miles, blue-white miles
of cotton, hiding old Uncle Vernon from the KKK. The clear

clean horizon doesn't show any chance of storm. Her own
glaucomatous eyes, dirt-brown like mine. I carry her for miles
in my blood—she is the weather—cold rain, thick in me, clears.

I Started Praying for You

Put my hands over
the cage of bones
above your heart.

I don't remember
exactly what I said.
You started to weep.

I know I said
God sees you
or *I see you.*

I said *Something
in your past
wants to be touched,*

healed. It was then
I knew I wanted
to marry you.

What is God to us now?
We stopped going
to church. In bed

our hands still
find each other
to send up

prayers like we
did that first night—
when I touched

the aching thing
inside the dip
of your chest.

After *Amistad*

Like the recurring iridescent sheen of green gantries floating over
the interstate reading: City of Pain 50 miles. I have avoided this moment,

watching these movies, slavery porn. I never wanted to take this exit—
Djimon Hounsou's face beaded, sopping with sweat and wild storm,

wet salt from the Atlantic. His persistent fingertips shredded with blood
from digging inside the wooden stomach of the ship, as if to break my brain

past the point of suture. Like a hammer, his heaving strikes and strikes
in between booming thunder and the dusty milk of the moon spilling light,

manacles jangling. The irises of his eyes, dark cinnamon concentrating
on the precious nail, now freed in the palm of his hand. I said to him,

Do you know how privileged you are to learn about this? This—
the slave trade, always looming, a phantom ship weaving the water's

dark deep. My husband's face flushed as his white skin blotched into a hue
of decanted merlot. The story is always the same story: black skin and money.

I am talking about the damage passed like a little gene, heirlooms of keloids
and torn cotton. I did not wipe the tears from my husband's sharp-white face.

His thin, soundless lips—so different from mine, like the face of the men
throwing my gorgeous people in chains to the sharks with such ferocity.

And when Cinqué yelled: *Give us free! Give us free!* I was already on my third drink, blurring. I do not know where I am from. It makes it difficult

to breathe—the fuzzy ache fingering the *dark*   country inside me—

Midnight to 3 A.M.

I glare

      at my husband snoring
      and think of mulatto house slaves,

      not all of them, just the ones
      that might have looked like me

      and were petrified, like me, to touch
      themselves, down there, down where

      it's burnt and swollen to worship
      that weak part of me that's cream,

      to hunger the part of me that's white
      matter, separated—the forgotten

      phonics of blood, thickening
      the room with red

      platelets. I close his mouth.
      I clap my hands. I turn him over

to stop
and start myself.

Rituals

what does it matter? —we made not doing it a wonder

∾ *Stuart Dybek*

The most dangerous game, for me,
is sex and syntax. Your hand, so familiar

and terrifying as family, reaches for my name,
and then my navel, which is a cup of hunger,

always in that order. My hand drags after loss,
after some inexact past. The wet mood lingers

erotic with the scent of a half-peeled orange,
broken by a nasty thumbnail. The moment clicks

and disappears again before we attempt release.
This hardened honey, this slow drip of joy.

Another spider approaches. And then I smash it.
Smearing gorgeous little guts like black lotion.

Strange how desire is greedy and silent in stasis.
Strange how two bodies can grow without branches.

And again. How do you diagram two broken bodies
without parsing? Without penetration? Is this still

what I want? Another year. Another sip of good
bourbon, neat and decadent. Something like a lock

unlatches. Another hard world approaches without
water. Another hard world approaches without fur.

Another hard world approaches and approaches
without punctuation, enters without sucking salt

from these two bodies, starved and pulsating
on the brink of so much touching and not touching.

I ache for grammar when it's bent and fluid.
I ache for him, for her, and then for myself, *always*

in that order, last in lust—I hum. I bang. I bite.
I touch myself, my many selves. If I whimper,

can I call it God? Oh God, please delay the verbs.
Once, in bed, you finally gave me what I wanted,

but I did not want it anymore. The whip cream
slid from your cool nipples in strings of white

tears. See, I'd already eaten so much sugar
that day. I was so full and sick of it.

Mixed Bitch

is allowed to love herself.

She wants to tell Nikky Finney
about her *beautiful black girl arms*
how they shimmer and shimmy in space—
making muscle songs of her tendons
and the dark matter beef.

Mixed Bitch wants to commission Kehinde Wiley.
She wants renaissance prints behind her mulatto skin,
gold lamé and a big ass frame inside the Frist
Museum.

She was caught between two allegiances, different,
yet the same. Herself. Her race. Race! The thing
that bound and suffocated her. Whatever steps
she took, or if she took none at all, something
would be crushed. Crushed?

Mixed Bitch don't know her Daddy.
Mixed Bitch don't know her Daddy.
Mixed   Bitch
          don't   know
her   Daddy.

But ain't she still allowed to love herself?

Mixed Bitch lets herself love—
the black inside: the white inside: the black of herself.

EPILOGUE

We tell beginnings: for the flesh and the answer,
or the look, the lake in the eye that knows,
for the despair that flows down in widest rivers,
cloud of home; and also the green tree of grace,
all in the leaf, in the love that gives us ourselves.

✑ Muriel Rukeyser

It is lonesome, yes. For we are the last of the loud.
Nevertheless, live.
Conduct your blooming in the noise and whip of the whirlwind.

✑ Gwendolyn Brooks

How to Find the Center of a Circle

x^2	$+ y^2$	$= r^2$
The first time	I	was called a *nigger*
with those	red hot	*g* sounds,
molten syllables	as searing lassos	around my neck
at a skating rink	they	like white spiders
spun around me	silking	a carousel of hate.
I didn't know	what	the word meant
but my body	blackened	wrong with heat.
Ugly	marked	a radius of shameful skin
as two white boys	taunted me	on roller skates,
they curved	the loop of	my circumference. I was
a little girl	crying	in the center of a circle—
felt	my selves	begin to double.
How	did I know	I was different?
I told the teacher	and she	put them in timeout.
But what about	the little girl	rolling away, struck
with the red	hot *g* sounds	ringing fire songs
in her ears?	You never forget	the first time
you are branded	with iron—	seared raw, permanent.

NOTES

Epigraphs:

> Roger Reeves, "Boy Removing Fleas," *King Me*
> Claudia Rankine, "[My brothers are notorious]," *Citizen: An American Lyric*
> Natasha Trethewey, "Pilgrimage," *Native Guard*
> Adrienne Rich, "What Kind of Times are These," from *Collected Poems: 1950–2012*
> Kevin Young, "Replicas," *To Repel Ghosts: Remixed from the Original Masters*
> Muriel Rukeyser, "Elegy in Joy [excerpt]," *Birds, Beasts, and Seas*
> Gwendolyn Brooks, "The Second Sermon on the Warpland," *In the Mecca*

"Cottonmouth" mentions Henry, John Berryman's blackface alter ego in *77 Dream Songs*, who often speaks in dialect as if in a minstrel show.

"Soil Horizon" excerpt from the Battle of Franklin Trust website.

"Conversation with Phillis Wheatley #14" is a fictional epistle from Obour Tanner (also spelled Abour and Arbour) 1750[?]–1835. She was Wheatley's only known correspondent of African descent. Wheatley's letters are all that survived their seven-year correspondence (approximately 1771/72–1778), and most of the letters can be viewed at the Massachusetts Historical Society online archive. I wanted to imagine, through persona, what Tanner's response might be to her dear friend, the first published African American female poet in America. I've also borrowed some of the diction from Wheatley's letters. Additionally, I was inspired by Katherine Clay Bassard's article, "The Daughters' Arrival: The Earliest Black Women's Writing Community," from *Callaloo* 19, no. 2 (Spring 1996). Bassard writes:

> Not only do these seven surviving letters force a necessary revision of the notion of a Phillis Wheatley completely isolated from other black women in community, but they also serve as a paradigm for the problematics and possibilities of early black women's writing community. As a broken, one-sided narrative in which letters are often sent back, delayed, or not received, large gaps in time—sometimes as much as four years—mark the desire for response with an ever-present deferral. Hand delivered by a third party (usually male), they are prone to violation and interception. Perhaps more importantly, each letter is sent "favd

by" someone, and "in care of" which marks the problematics of ownership for black women slaves, a qualification which framed even their most intimate attempts to communicate with each other.

Dear Reader, I thought about cutting #7 in "Ways to Be Saved," due to Kanye West's recent shenanigans, but ultimately I decided to leave the poem as is. For more thoughts on Kanye, be sure to read Ta-Nehisi Coates's brilliant essay in the *Atlantic* titled "I'm Not Black, I'm Kanye: Kanye West Wants Freedom—White Freedom."

"800 Days: Libation" is an elegy for Kalief Browder, who was imprisoned as a sixteen-year-old on Rikers Island for three years without ever being convicted of a crime. He grappled with mental health issues that were largely due to the extreme physical and psychological distress endured during his time in solitary confinement as well as trial set backs, all while declaring his innocence. Two years after finally being released, Browder took his own life. *Time: The Kalief Browder Story* is a six-episode documentary television miniseries that aired on Spike TV in 2017.

Apollo was the first ballet in a series of collaborations between famed choreographer George Balanchine and composer Igor Stravinsky. *Orpheus* and *Agon*, the subsequent ballets, would complete the trilogy. Referring to *Agon*, Arthur Mitchell, an African American dancer, has said, "My skin color against hers, it became part of the choreography." Further insight about *Agon* from Joan Acocella in *The New Yorker*:

> Arthur Mitchell has said that when he and Adams first performed the "Agon" duet, it looked different from today's renditions. For dancers of that period, the steps were very difficult, he said, and Adams was afraid that she wouldn't be able to do them. This made her seem vulnerable. She might also have been nervous about the duet's sexual frankness. In a lift, she goes into a front-facing split that I doubt had ever been seen on a ballet stage before. But combined with this bluntness was a strange, hushed tenderness. In 1956, Balanchine's wife, Tanaquil Le Clercq—who, with Adams, was his lead ballerina—was stricken with polio. He left the company for a year, to stay by her side. He spent hours doing physical therapy with her. When he returned to N.Y.C.B., he made "Agon," in which

Mitchell often takes Adams's feet and legs in his hands, guiding them, placing them. The duet, then, was a strange package of fear and intimacy and eroticism, and all this was made more daring—or in 1957 it was—by the fact that Mitchell is black and Adams was white.

"The Rime of Nina Simone" is based loosely after "The Rime of the Ancient Mariner" by Samuel Taylor Coleridge. Several lines are borrowed from these various sources:

Federico García Lorca, "from the furthest habitations of my blood," from "Theory and Play of the Duende"

Jonathan Edwards, "Sinners in the Hands of an Angry God"

Borrowed inspiration from several passages in *I Put a Spell on You: The Autobiography of Nina Simone* with Stephen Cleary

William Wordsworth, ". . . these beauteous forms" and "(In hours of weariness, sensations sweet, felt in the blood, and felt along the heart.)," from "Lines Composed a Few Miles above Tintern Abbey, On Revisiting the Banks of the Wye during a Tour. July 13, 1798," *Lyrical Ballads*

Robert Hayden, "Jesus   Saviour   Pilot   Me," from "Middle Passage"

Emily Dickinson, "You cannot put a Fire out—" 530, excerpt:
>A Thing that can ignite
>Can go, itself, without a Fan—
>Upon the slowest Night—

An epigraph that was not included, but was central to the inspiration reverberating throughout "The Rime of Nina Simone" is as follows:

>Now, it is not addressed primarily to white people. Though it does not put you down in any way. It simply ignores you. For my people need all the inspiration and love that they can get.
>
>> ∾ *Nina Simone*, during her introduction to the civil rights anthem, "Young, Gifted, and Black," written for Lorraine Hansberry, at the Philharmonic Hall in New York live album recording for *Black Gold*, 1969.

"BBHMM" is an acronym for the song "Bitch Better Have My Money" by Rihanna.

Black hair references for white people in "Where the Fired Body Is Porous" are as follows:

> Type 3c curls resemble tight corkscrews and are approximately the circumference of a pencil or straw. Type 3c hair tends to be higher in density and coarser than type 2 or 3 hair, giving it more volume. Type 3c curls are finer in texture, though packed tightly together on the head. (Source: www.naturallycurly.com)

> It's common that there is more coarseness in the back, than in the front. We call that back area "the kitchen." I never found out why we call it that. I just remember my mother, aunts and grandmothers doing my hair saying things like "we got to straighten out that kitchen" when going through my hair with hot combs. . . . That brings me to "pressing hair." So basically hair oil/grease was applied along the hairline and to the scalp. Thick metal combs were placed on the open gas flame in the kitchen. Sometimes the handles were loose from so much grease and use. Granny grabs the comb by the wooden handle and tells me to hold down my ears. This is difficult because I'm sweating, my head is greasy, and my ears are now slippery. So the object of Granny's game is to get the crazy hot comb as close to my scalp as possible, without burning me. This is all to straighten my hair. The smell is awful. What does it smell like? Burnt hair and grease. Go figure. Oh the grease popping. The holding down of my ears so they wouldn't get burned. (Excerpt from Blackerberry.wordpress.com)

"Unbound" alludes to these various texts:

> The reference to Nikky Finney is after her speech, "A Young Black Woman Shimmy & Shakes a Flagpole and Finally Brings the Confederate Flag Down After One Hundred Years: Thoughts on Climbing, Not Waiting on the Calvary, Faith, and Manners, in the Contemporary South," Vanderbilt University Divinity School, Cole Lectures, October 8, 2015.

> She was caught between two allegiances, different, yet the same. Herself. Her race. Race! The thing that bound and suffocated her. Whatever steps she took, or if she took none at all, something would be crushed. (Nella Larson, *Passing*)

ACKNOWLEDGMENTS

Thank you to the following journals where these poems, sometimes under different titles and forms, have appeared:

"Nashville," *The New Yorker*; "Cottonmouth," "I Started Praying for You," & "Mother Driving Away after Christmas," *American Poetry Review*; "After *Orpheus*" & "After *Apollo*," *Arkansas International*; "Conversation with Phillis Wheatley #2," *Blueshift Journal*; "Midnight to 3 A.M.," *Boaat Journal*; "Freelove in Retrograde," *Crab Orchard Review*; "After *Agon*" & "In the Middle of Things," *Eleven Eleven Literary Journal*; "Tim," *Frontier Poetry*; "Conversation with Phillis Wheatley #1" & "After *Amistad*," *Grist Journal*; "Where the Fired Body Is Porous," *Grist Journal Online*; "Cross/Bite," *HEArt Online Journal*; "Self-Portrait as First Kiss," *Indiana Review*; "Dead Bug" & "First Tree, at Church Camp," *Iron Horse Literary Review*; "BBHMM" & "*Dutchman* in Reverse," *The Journal*; "How to Find the Center of a Circle," *Muzzle Magazine*; "Rituals," *New England Review*; "Ode to the Only Living Object that Survived," "After Water, Recovered Letter from Obour Tanner 1," "Self Portrait as Hannah Peace at The Cotton Eyed Joe in Knoxville, TN," & "I Started My Period in Childcare, Eleven-years-old," *Obsidian*; "800 Days: Libation," *Poem-a-Day* featured on Poets.org; "Soil Horizon," Poets.org; "The Ayes Have It," *Raven Chronicles*; "Ways to be Saved," *The Rumpus*; "Eve of Janus Debutante Ball," *Sewanee Review*; "The Rime of Nina Simone," *Southern Cultures*; "Bear Witness," *Thrush*.

"Bear Witness," "How to Find the Center of a Circle," and "Unbound" previously appeared in *Equilibrium*, selected by Afaa Michael Weaver for the 2016 Frost Place Chapbook Competition. "The Ayes Have It" was also featured in short film for Motionpoems. Poems that appeared in *Obsidian* won the 2017 Furious Flower's Gwendolyn Brooks Centennial Poetry Prize. Please note the title change for "Recovered Letter from Obour Tanner 1" to "Conversation with Phillis

Wheatley #14." "Soil Horizon" won the Academy of American Poets Vanderbilt University Prize, judged by T. R. Hummer. Please note the title change for "Eve of Janus Debutante Ball" to "Conversation with Phillis Wheatley #7." "How to Find the Center of a Circle" was selected by Kazim Ali for the 2016 Best of the Net Anthology. "Tim" won the *Frontier Poetry* Open Prize. "BBHMM" was selected for *The Pushcart Prize XLIII: Best of the Small Presses* (forthcoming 2019).

My mother, Verna Knight, thank you for your sacrifice and love. My second mother, Lisa Waters. To my incredibly loving and supporting mother-in-law, Jodie Clark. My first creative writing teacher, Bill Brown, thank you for fostering my growth as a writer with books and steady encouragement for over eighteen years. To my Auntie, Joycene, and John James. My best friend, Alex Kanski, my constant.

Deep love for my Nashville literary family, especially Ciona Rouse, Kate Parrish, Kendra DeColo, Jeff Hardin, Allison Inman, Leslie LaChance, Chance Chambers, Joshua Moore, Christina Stoddard, TJ Jarrett, Gary McDowell, Elizabeth Townsend, Parnassus Books, Porch Writers' Collective (Susannah Felts and Katie McDougall), Ryne Driscoll, Matthew Johnstone, Joseph and Cindi Seward Powell, Page Regan with T.Y.M.E., Chapter 16, Nashville Scene, Charlie Hickerson with *Native* magazine, Chuck Beard, Christine Hall, Joyce Sohl with Scarritt Bennett Center, and too many duende-drenched people to name.

Endless gratitude to Kate Daniels, my invaluable thesis advisor, mentor, and dear friend. Special thanks and admiration to the rest of the Creative Writing faculty at Vanderbilt for your continued wisdom, crucial edits, and mentorship (and now friendship), especially Mark Jarman, Rick Hilles, Beth Bachmann, and Nancy Reisman. To the rest of my Vandy family near and far: Jesse Bertron, Kelsey Norris, Donika Kelly, Mark Haslam, Max McDonough, Sohpia Stid, Mary Somerville, Rita Bullwinkel, Katie Foster & Tim, Anders Carlson-Wee, Edgar Kunz, Dan Haney, Simon Han, Anna Silverstein, Carla Diaz, Tatiana McInnis,

Cydnee Devereaux, Stephanie Davis, Samuel Rutter, Lisa Muloma, Lee Conell, Matthew Baker, Freya Sachs, Destiny Birdsong, Alicia Marie Brandewie, Lisa Dordal, René Colehour, and with immense love for Dr. Houston A. Baker Jr. and Dr. Charlotte Pierce-Baker.

To my passionately brilliant and supportive UW-Madison fellows: Oliver Baez Bendorf, Leila Chatti, Tia Clark, and Marta Evans, such deep appreciation for our frozen year of love together and always. To our amazing director, Amaud Jamaul Johnson, thanks for showing me Ellison's "jagged grain." Special shout-out to the rest of the amazing faculty, MFA cohort, and fellows past and present, especially Derrick Austin and Natalie Eilbert.

Big love for the continued support and brilliance of Kaveh Akbar, Gabrielle Calvocoressi, Patricia Smith, Ross Gay, Robert Hass, Carl Phillips, Lyrae van Clief-Stefanon, Charif Shanahan, Ilya Kaminsky, Honorée Fanonne Jeffers, Fatimah Asghar, Alex Dimitrov, Ada Limón, Noah Stetzer, David Tomas Martinez, Jenny Johnson, Phillip B. Williams, Kevin Young, Paul Muldoon, Hannah Aizenman, Eduardo C. Corral, Rick Barot, Marilyn Kallet, Jason McCall, Peter LaBerge, Eileen Rush, Elizabeth Yandel, Lindsay Ambrose, Molly McCully Brown, Tyler Mills, Jan Verberkmoes, Melissa Johnson (and the rest of our amazing 2016 Sewanee workshop), A. H. Jerriod Avant, Kelly Forsythe, Paige Lewis, Mahogany L. Browne, Cortney Lamar Charleston, Geffrey Davis, Jessica Jacobs, Mallory Imler Powell, Allison Joseph, and Jon Tribble. All of my amazing students. Your continued support and celebration keep me buoyed and enthusiastically inspired.

Thanks for the incredible support from the Furious Flower Poetry Center (Dr. Joanne V. Gabbin, Lauren K. Alleyne, and Karen Risch Mott), Maudelle Driskel and The Frost Place, Ross White and Bull City Press, Metro Arts' THRIVE micro-funding program, Rattle Poetry Prize, *Frontier Poetry* Open Prize, Poetry

Asylum, New Harmony Writers Workshop, Sewanee Writers' Conference, Sewanee Young Writers' Conference, and the Bread Loaf Writers' Conference.

I'm grateful to the University of Pittsburgh Press, and especially to Ed Ochester for selecting my book. I appreciate all the help and support from Peter Kracht, Maria Sticco, and Alex Wolfe. To my new Pitt Press fam: Nate Marshall, Julian Randall, Shauna Barbosa, and Rickey Laurentiis. We lit.

And you.

God.